Lord Help Your People but Please Start with Me

Alonda Cousizan-Cooper

Published By: Heaven's Press Publishing ™®
Alonda Cooper
– P.O. Box 2768 Slidell, LA 70459
Phone: 985-646-2354 Website: www.alondacooper.com

Scripture quotations are used primarily from the King James Version of the
Holy Bible. Unless otherwise noted.
Scripture quotations marked (NLT) or (AMP) are taken from the New Living
Translation and Amplified Bible online bibles provided by Bible Gateway.

Acknowledgements & Thanks

Honor is due to those who obeyed God and prophesied the word over my life, as well as, prayed and believed for the prophetic words to come into fruition. To My Spiritual Mothers & Mentors – Aunt Bernstein Faciane, Prophetess Deborah Winston, and Mother Rosemary McDoneal. I love you all more than you know and I am eternally grateful that our paths crossed.

To Pastor Samuel R. Blakes and his beautiful wife First Lady, Stacey W. Blakes. I appreciate you for your contribution to the kingdom of God and for allowing me to stumble, fumble, falter, and fail as I served you guys. Thanks for teaching me not to allow my hang ups to become my hangouts. I have evolved from the lessons learned while sitting and serving under your tutelage. Pastor R. C. Blakes, Jr thanks for the encouragement through receiving the prophetic words that the Lord spoke through little ole' me.

Those who heard the voice of God and embraced my ministry Thank You – Elder D'Evelyn Bartie, Pastors Chris & Felicia Dexter, Min. Cynthia Dixon, Prophetess Beverly

Lewis, Pastor Peggy Ratcliff, Apostle Sterling Winston, Sr., and the late Prophetess Gwendolyn Cotton, Thank you for your prayer covering. Aunt Gloria Tate thanks for encouraging me to walk worthy.

To my dear sweet cousin the famous Sweet Opal the greatest personal encourager on this side of heaven. I appreciate you for keeping it real with me and keeping me focused on the fixed fight at all times. I cannot tell you how many countless times you have given me life by one of your phone calls. I am determined to stay 'True To It!'

To my parents Alonzo and Dianne Cousizan thanks so much for introducing me to JESUS CHRIST the LOVE OF MY LIFE! The Anointed One is the reason I have made it through. I am truly blessed and highly favored because of your teachings and example. I can only hope that you are proud of your eldest child.

1st Fruit Prayer Connection – Thanks for all of your prayers, love, and support!

His Will Worship Center – You know what we always say "Expectation Plus Participation Equals God's Manifestation!" This is just the beginning for us all. I thank you for believing in me and I pray that each of you fight the good fight of faith so that you may WIN BY FORCE.

I LOVE YOU ALL!

Special Thanks

To the other Love of my life
My Husband, My Friend, and My Pastor, Vernell Cooper,
Jr - THANK YOU My Honey You're My Shining Star! You
are certainly every girls dream but I bless heaven that I
am your only dream. Thanks for listening and believing
in me each time I said I heard God say. You have truly
loved me as Christ loved the church – Unconditionally!!!

You are simply the best and if I haven't told you
lately that I love you...HONEY I LOVE YOU!

Dedication

I present this book as a First Fruit Offering back to the one who inspired it – Holy Spirit.

I dedicate this book to my beautiful daughters. To my oldest Alexis Dianne, THANKS BUNCHES for being mommies' sounding board. It is with sincere hope that you caught what was taught.

I have made every effort to teach you to have Faith in God, Love in spite of and that it was imperative to believe in your calling and your dreams. From the day you were born I set out to groom you into classiness, success, ful-filled prophesy and to receive your promises all which would make our Father Proud, Jesus Shine, & Holy Spirit Embraced. I am a proud mother and I pray that you are a proud daughter. I promised you when you were just a baby that I would become and be the example that you could follow. I Love You to Life and for Life! I am looking for-ward to seeing you in the future, as well as, reading both you and your sister's first published works.

Netta Chanel, my baby girl I didn't forget about you, but you've read and heard what I said and with this book I impart to both of you an entrepreneurial anointing and a pen of a ready writer. I not only love you but I love you more than you know!

My princess and my angel start succeeding NOW! Remember you must write the vision so you can watch it unfold before your eyes.

Introduction

Uggghh...You know what, just stick a fork in me because I'm done. Yeah I said, it I am done. I'm done with so many Human Beings being crooked, conniving, and callous. I no longer want to deal with the impatient nor insolent. Oh, and I can't forget all the ingrates I've encountered.

I am done with being angry with the world, done with being undisciplined, unstable and being double minded. I am done with being treated like I am the curse when truth is I am the blessing.

Have you ever had one of those unending days or seasons in life where everything irks your nerves? The energy around you is negative, the people you come in contact with zap you and in some cases their frustration, oppression, and mediocrity slaps you? I mean every social network post or tweet you read is someone trying to tell someone off with the audacity of using GOD along with the blasphemous language of satan. Better yet you become disgruntled because you read post from disgruntled posters commenting on what they have absolutely no fact, truth, expertise or understanding on. Well, you know what? I am tired of it and Lord I want you to Help Your People but PLEASE start with me....

"Uh-uh Wow!" is exactly what I uttered when those words, Lord Help Your People; but Please Start With Me, came up out of my spirit. Immediately I began to examine myself and tried to figure out why I was in this miserable season of vexation and stagnation.

I began to question myself as to how is it that I feel this way and why on earth am I so upset with everyone to boiling point.

Instead of me being ready for the world I am mad with the world. As I pondered in my self-reflection, Holy Spirit gently whispered to me this scripture from the Holy Bible· *"And why beholdest thou the mote that is in thy brother's eye, but considerest not the beam that is in thine own eye?"* ~ *Matthew 7:3*. So it really is me OH LORD standing in the need of prayer and deliverance?! Tears began to stream down my face as I prayed and cried out for supernatural assistance from these horrible irritable, and embarrassing demon manifestations. I begin to employ the help of my Advocate, my Guide, my Teacher, my Helper, and my Comforter Holy Spirit so that I would be able to assist others, thus the authoring of this book.

"But when the Father sends the Advocate as my rep-resentative — that is, the Holy Spirit — He will teach you everything and will remind you of everything I have told you."

~ John 14:26(NLT)

Chapter 1

My Heart- The Method

"Create in me a clean heart, O God; and renew
a right spirit within me." ~ Psalm 51:10

❈

"Where do I need to start and what exactly do I need to do to rid myself of these burdens and this ache in my heart?" I asked my teacher Holy Spirit and He said give me permission to CREATE and RENEW a right spirit in you. That's easy enough I thought. Okay then Holy Spirit, permission granted. Not only do we have to give Him permission to Create and Renew but we also have to follow His method of doing things.

His method can be found in Luke chapter 6 beginning at verse 27 and ending at verse 38.

*But I say unto you which hear, Love your enemies, do good to them which hate you,...***Okay***...Bless them that curse you, and pray for them which despitefully use you...***Alright*** And unto him that smiteth thee on the one cheek offer also*

1

the other; and him that taketh away thy cloak forbid not to take thy coat also....'**Wait a minute! I can love them and I will even pray for them, but is it really necessary to turn my cheeks and give up my belongings?'** I asked. He simply replied you cannot do part of it.

You are not loving if you are not giving and forgiving.

In order for anyone to become the new Creation, their old habits of thinking and doing must change. Where you used to hate those that hate, I want you to love. Where your old occupation was to curse along with those who cursed others out, your new occupation is going to become intercession. I wasn't exactly sure what good this was going to do but, hey I sought your help so let me see where this is going. Then, He hit me with the rest of my prescription for a genuine heart change.

[30] *Give to every man that asketh of thee; and of him that taketh away thy goods ask them not again.* [31] *And as ye would that men should do to you, do ye also to them likewise...* **Speechless I had no words at this point.** [32] *For if ye love them which love you, what thank have ye? for sinners also love those that love them.* [33] *And if ye do good to them which do good to you, what thank have ye? for sinners also do even the same.* [34] *And if ye lend to them of whom ye hope to receive, what thank have ye? for sinners also lend to sinners, to receive as much again.* [35] *But love ye your enemies, and do good, and lend, hoping for nothing again;...* **Jesus you're joking right?** *and your reward shall be great, and ye shall be the children*

of the Highest: **...Oh never mind I do get something in return**... *for he is kind unto the unthankful and to the evil...* **Whew THANK You Lord!**[36] *Be ye therefore merciful, as your Father also is merciful.*[37] *Judge not, and ye shall not be judged: condemn not, and ye shall not be condemned: forgive, and ye shall be forgiven:*[38] *Give, and it shall be given unto you; good measure, pressed down, and shaken together, and running over, shall men give into your bosom. For with the same measure that ye mete withal it shall be measured to you again.*

I bet you're thinking, "man surely it doesn't take all that". Well if you didn't think it, I'll be honest I sure did. At first glance I was like, I am already sick and tired of being sick and tired & you're gonna give me a mouthful of scriptures to swallow that require me to do consistent and random acts of kindness for those who are abusive, boisterous, belligerent, critical, clueless, nasty, thoughtless, unsuspecting, and undeserving? You get my drift because the list can go on and on. I was like, "shucks Holy Spirit, it's easier for me to just stay the way I am because I know how to do that. In fact, truth be told, I am exactly what I have been complaining and murmuring about and I am named amongst the aforementioned list I rattled off" (Especially clueless). "Lord, I really need you to Help Me," I uttered.

I looked at the scriptures again and convinced myself that this wasn't so bad and it's actually a win-win situation if I would just put it into practice. I got the impression that it was high time I became the difference and learn to walk at a higher standard. Besides, what is the point of being a part of something that is exactly like everything? I am on the quest to understand our peculiarity in Christendom.

Look at these passages of scriptures with me again and you will begin to recognize that Jesus was teaching what I call the importance of ING. The suffix ING is simply the process connected to a specified action. Jesus gives us specific strategic reactions to every evil action, no matter if it is the obvious evil or covert.

Loving, Doing, Forgiving, Giving and Receiving.

"But I say unto you which hear, Love your enemies, do good to them which hate you,
Bless them that curse you, and pray for
them which despitefully use you.
And unto him that smiteth thee on the one cheek
offer also the other; and him that taketh
away thy cloak forbid not to take thy coat also." ~ Luke 6:27

In order for Holy Spirit to do a complete work in me and for me to be released from the chains of my pain, I had to become more Loving, Doing, Forgiving, Giving and Receiving. This meant I had to genuinely love those who betrayed me, forgive those who molested me, raped and rejected me. I had to be a blessing to those who spoke word curses against me and didn't even know me. Then it was imperative that I turn around and pray for those who despitefully abused and used me. (Yes I have been there and done all that; got all of the T-shirts honey!)

Point Blank, I had to <u>quit giving justifiable</u> reasons why I couldn't and why I shouldn't receive my breakthrough to JOY unspeakable.

Whenever I would become agitated in my process in Luke chapter six, Holy Spirit would gently nudge me and say you solicited my help and gave your word that you would surrender all to the process. So it doesn't matter if they took your kindness for weakness. It should no longer be your concern how they used your gifts & talents for their gain, nor how your loyalty to the relationship or fellowship is now disdained. Now is not the time to become coy and show reluctance to the commitment. You must focus intently on Loving, Doing, Forgiving, and Giving so you can do some Receiving. In order to see the liberty in the rewards of Love, Peace, Joy, Gentleness, Goodness, Kindness, Patience, Faithfulness and Self-Control, Luke chapter six has to become your personal life vision, mission, confession and lifestyle. A good lifestyle might I add...A LIFESTYLE with BENEFITS.

You know it's not just me, but many of us in the Body of Christ need what we call a 'rude awakening' of the fact that GOD IS LOVE period. In first John chapter four verse eight it says,

"But anyone who does not love does not know God, for God is love." ~ I John 4:8

Well the scripture is clear, I ain't nothing but a liar (It's not good grammar but you understand). How can I, Alonda, say I know God, when I am upset with the world both sinners and saints? I mean really every time I think of certain folk who have crushed me, ignored me, lied on me and pretended to be for me I get this painful heavy pressure in my chest, lump in my throat and tears swell up in my eyes. How can I say I know God when I am so easily vexed and ready to throw in my towel, as well as, the towel of anyone who provokes me to become irritable? Hold up stop the presses because my heart just skipped a beat! I must pause and pray because I don't know about anyone else but when Jesus comes I surely do not want to be told depart from me you worker of iniquity I don't know you and you don't know me.

The more I pen my thoughts to paper the more sensitive I am becoming to the fact that we really are not just in a dying world but our world is dying because of our putrid hate for others and ourselves. Anyway, it's high time I remedy myself of being a professing Christian who instead of keeping the promise to convince and compel others to come to Christ. I fall in the lineup with the crooked, conniving, and callous. Rather than being thankful, tolerant and imperturbable. I too had become the object of my frustration, I had allowed the infiltration of Anger, Bitterness, Hurt, Crudeness & Rudeness all of what bothered me about others had slowly turned me into a heartless and impatient ingrate...In some church arenas right through here they would Say PREACH...I don't know what it is but we like to be told off by the preachers by saying that he/she keeps it real. But you know what if you can't say amen say ouch. O-o-ouch!!

I realized that as we allow Holy Spirit to use the word to construct and reconstruct our hearts, we reproduce spiritual thinking and habits like our Father in heaven. My Soul would receive rest from the anguish of both the actions of myself as well as others. I came to a quick understanding that by submitting to His heart transplant that I would not only become better and no longer be bitter, but I would be one step closer to being and seeing the change I desired to see in others.

Let us pray
Father,
Thank you for loving me, doing for me, giving to me and receiving me. Now Holy Spirit teach me to be just like Father. In Jesus Christ Name,
Amen.

Chapter 2

A Re NEW ed You - Beam of Unforgiveness

"Give, and it shall be given unto you; good measure, pressed down, and shaken together, and running over, shall men give into your bosom. For with the same measure that ye mete withal it shall be measured to you again." ~ Luke 6:38

❧

I know this scripture is printed on church envelopes around the church world and quoted often for the offering appeal, but you rarely hear anyone speak of the preceding words of Jesus admonishing us not to condemn others, give up resentment and acquit. If we would just let folk off the hook, Father would measure back to us more grace when and whilst we are screwing up. In other words, we receive the compassion of Christ's love and a renewed person's love pressed down, shaken together, run over into our bosom. Instead of the lump in my throat and pressure on my chest, I will experience forgiveness as I am giving it out. Better yet, we would begin to experience the power of God causing our enemies to be at peace with us. This renewal system of Loving, Doing, Forgiving and Giving affords me the opportunity to not only mature but to also exemplify the very nature of the Trinity; the Father, Son, & Holy Spirit, as well as, receive that much more grace abounding toward me. If you haven't notice yet, this here sister, daughter, mother, wife, prayer warrior, business woman, and Prophet, and Pastor needs some Grace coming her way. Not just the new grace I wake up to, but the grace that I am rewarded because I practice the principles of the word of God. Oh yeah, your girl has quickly turned into a cheek turning somebody! **It's the best and simplest math I've ever done. I Do, I Give and He Does & He Gives exceedingly abundantly more than I could think or ask.** Yes, I am willing to invest in myself too because the return is unyielding. Hey, don't hate on me because I love the kingdom benefits and perks of being a follower (doer) of Christ!

"Moreover the law entered that the offense might abound. But where sin abounded, grace abounded much more," ~ Romans 5:20

I could no longer lay awake at night pondering all the whys. Why all the jealousy over my anointing? Why did they betray me? Why can't they see I am a great person? Why did they pretend to be my friend? Or in some instances, why can't they forgive me and let bygones be bygones? Maybe, just maybe, it was the probability that I was lying to myself saying that I had forgiven them when really I hadn't. Hopefully, if you've made it this far in the book you are beginning to see what needs to transpire in your own life. If you really want to DO YOU to the fullest you're definitely going to have to Let It Go. Let go of pride and let go of the fear of being humiliated ever again and Give-Give-Give. Give love until it no longer hurts you but it stirs you and steers you; Pray until you are no longer cantankerous; Turn your cheek until the spirit of error is corrected in the offender and you the offended.

You are probably wondering how I overcame and just how did I move forward in allowing Holy Spirit to CREATE AND RENEW ME. Well we are on the same page because although He had given me the method, often times I did not know how to employ the methods. Boy Oh Boy! This was tough especially the closer I drew to God. I found the closer I drew to Him my mind and spirit needed more purging than I anticipated. I had so many unresolved issues from my past. **I had absolutely no idea how much junk was actually in my trunk covering up my treasures.** The junk of my upbringing, relationships, friendships, and choices had become templates, firewalls and viruses in my life that were both oppressing and impeding me from a full life of success, joy, and peace.

How I Did It and How I Do It

First He led me to a passage of scripture in James 4:6, *"But he gives us even <u>more</u> grace to stand against such evil desires. As the Scriptures say, "God opposes the proud but favors the humble."* Then I remembered a scripture in James chapter 1 verse 5 that said, *"If you need wisdom, ask our generous God, and he will give it to you. He will not rebuke you for asking.* So how did I overcome? It's simple, I ASKED. Here, you try it; Father I want to obey your word in every situation and I need your wisdom in employing your methods of loving, doing, giving and receiving, so that I do not come across as desperate, needy, or motive driven. Give me wisdom that will ensure my actions, as well as intentions, are always pure in heart. My only agendas are pleasing you Father and to receive my breakthrough, healing, deliverance, and to become a FAVOR MAGNET. I humble myself in giving you permission to remove all urges of pride and prejudices in this process of receiving HELP and becoming the help you have called me to be. In Jesus Christ Name, Amen.

That's it, we're going to need to embrace wisdom, meekness and perseverance to obtain the help that we want and so desperately need to be helpers of each other.

"Blessed are the meek: for they shall inherit the earth." ~ *Matthew 5:5*

"Blessed are the pure in heart: for they shall see God. ~ *Matthew 5:8*

I am so glad that I cried out for HELP.

Chapter 3

Woman Overboard ...Just Die Already

❧

As I alluded in previous chapters in my come to Jesus meeting, I found out that I had let the actions of others change me. The spirit of God began to reveal to me that I was an angry, double minded, running scared prophet like the prophets Jonah and Elijah. He also let it be known that I had become undisciplined, as well as, both Covetous and Jealous myself...yeah He kept dropping bombshells on me because He wanted me to just die to myself. He wanted me to overcome this old carnal flesh. Because the carnal mind is enmity, against God: for it is not subject to the law of God, neither indeed can be. You see the word of God clearly states that the carnal mind is enmity, animosity against God: and guess what it was becoming painfully clear just how much of an overhaul that my mind needed. My mind was functioning in hatred & hostility and causing me to be in SIN. How can I say I love God and Hate?

"So you also must consider yourselves dead to sin and alive to God in Christ Jesus. Let not sin therefore reign in your mortal body, to make you obey its passions. Do not present your members to sin as instruments for unrighteousness, but present yourselves to God as those who have been brought from death to life, and your members to God as instruments for righteousness. For sin will have no dominion over you, since you are not under law but under grace." This writing of the Apostle Paul in Romans chapter six verses 11-14 brought not only conviction but convincing to my heart that I needed to just die already especially for me to function in the office in which I was born into of the Prophet.

Yes SIN no one is really talking about sin or if they do they only speak of what they call big sin you know the obvious such as fornication, adultery, homosexuality, drinking, cussing, and stealing. Sure the Apostle Paul list the so called Big sins in first Corinthians chapter six but named among them are others all of which will keep us from inheriting the Kingdom of God.

But in addition to this what about the seven things God hates in Proverbs chapter six. *"These six things the LORD HATES, YES, SEVEN ARE AN ABOMINATION TO HIM: A proud look, A lying tongue, Hands that shed innocent blood, A heart that devises wicked plans, Feet that are swift in running to evil, A false witness who speaks lies, And one who sows discord among brethren."*

It goes on to tell us that we were made right with God when we called on the name of the Lord Jesus Christ and by the Spirit of our God. We have to hold on to the fact that we are new creatures in Christ old things are passed away. We cannot stay in nor should we revert back to our BC before Christ days. We must press toward the mark of the prize which was also in Christ Jesus. Hold up, not inherit the Kingdom of God. Don't believe me just read it for yourself.

"Don't you realize that those who do wrong will not inherit the Kingdom of God? Don't fool yourselves. Those who indulge in sexual sin, or who worship idols, or commit adultery, or are male prostitutes, or practice homosexuality, or are thieves, or Covetous greedy people, or drunkards, or are abusive, or cheat people—none of these will inherit the Kingdom of God.[11] *Some of you were once like that. But you were cleansed; you were made holy; you were made right with God by calling on the name of the Lord Jesus Christ and by the Spirit of our God." ~ 1 Corinthians 6:9-11*

Yeah, I hear you as you are reading this saying *"Lord Help Your people but please start with me."* Well here's some help for you just read about the Grace. **It's not seminary science His Grace is simply the favor that gives you the ability to be triumphant over sin.**

Let us take a look at the Prophet Jonah...

Jonah 1:1-2 - The Lord gave this message to Jonah son of Amittai: "Get up and go to the great city of Nineveh. Announce my judgment against it because I have seen how wicked its people are."

Like Jonah He'd give me a word, instruction, and correction that I felt was an inconvenience because for starters it required that I had to Get up and Go. Secondly, it required me to be bothered with those wicked people. Those who had jacked me up in the first place. Besides why do I need to travel to tell them you gone kill 'em. Just do it without warning they deserve it gone strike 'em dead. I give you permission to do it. This statement alone lets you see that I had become self-righteous and narrow-minded. Neither Jonah nor I were any different from the Ninevhites that God wanted to use us to warn that their transgressions, iniquities and sin had earned them a death sentence. Oh yeah it was horrible to realize my heart had not only become wicked but the demon manifestations were getting worse each time I'd go purchase a ticket to try to run away from God. Boy Oh boy was this a difficult dilemma for me because the personality of the Prophet is to see in black & white only. There is no gray with us. But the problem was not my eyesight it was my heart. I do not care what your position, function, office, title or how many alphabets you have behind your name. If you are not demonstrating your obedience to God through compassion and love there is the strong possibility that you will end up receiving a death penalty. Trust me when I say you will suffer a painstaking slow spiritual, emotional and relational deaths all prior to your inevitable physical death. You will surely become the worst kind of outcast; the kind that no one wants to be around or to be bothered with including yourself. Bring your body into subjection so that you would not be as the Apostle Paul wrote a castaway.

"But I keep under my body, and bring it into subjection: lest that by any means, when I have preached to others, I myself should be a castaway." ~ 1 Corinthians 9:27

Jonah bought a ticket for a cruise ship to hide. My ticket was oftentimes a drink, marijuana, or a ticket to finding love in the wrong places that of the comfort of a looser. Only to find myself in a ferocious storm as Jonah but no matter which ticket or tickets I purchased I still could not drown out His voice, His dreams, His visions, or His promptings. (By the way all this was a part of my prophetic training) With each ticket purchase it was taking me down deeper into disobedience, depression and disparity.

Let me tell you the worse ticket to buy is the 'Try to Fit in Ticket.' Because once those you are trying to fit in with cast lots and recognize your difference, your anointing and that you are an imposter who serves a different God or that you are SAVED FOR REAL. They are surely going to confront and interrogate you just as the sailors did Jonah.

"Then the crew cast lots to see which of them had offended the gods and caused the terrible storm. When they did this, the lots identified Jonah as the culprit. "Why has this awful storm come down on us?" they demanded. "Who are you? What is your line of work? What country are you from? What is your nationality?" ~ Jonah 1:7 - 8

First of all them spirits want to be left alone they don't want any part of God they are complacent in their wickedness serving other gods or serving God halfheartedly. Secondly, they are going to question you to see if you are authentic or not. Look at the scripture above the first question they asked was why? Let me pause and help a Nabi (young) prophet right here. In your ministry function people expect you to know Why, When, and How. After all this is their only reason for seeking out a True Prophet. As you mature and depending on your level of grace in functioning as a prophet you will be able to answer these questions with accuracy at the sole discretion and leading of Holy Spirit.

I found out quickly that interrogation was an integral part of my prophetic training. I learned that at all times I had to be honest with myself, others and God. True prophets can't live a lie, be lie, nor should they be telling lies. After all we are the mouthpieces of God. This is why you have to throw yourself overboard you have to continually die. No If's, Ands or But's about it.

If you are believer of Jesus Christ you cannot negate or escape the dying process.

I'm telling you your best bet is to scream out throw me overboard like Jonah and just die already.

> *"Throw me into the sea, Jonah said,*
> *and it will become calm again.*
> *I know that this terrible storm is all my fault."- Jonah 1:12*

Now where was I...Oh lastly whenever a person with a genuine anointing is around something happens in the atmosphere, a circumstance and regional vicinity.

> *"Then they cried out to the Lord, Jonah's God. "O Lord," they pleaded, "don't make us die for this man's sin. And don't hold us responsible for his death. O Lord, you have sent this storm upon him for your own good reasons." Then the sailors picked Jonah up and threw him into the raging sea, and the storm stopped at once! The sailors were awestruck by the Lord's great power, and they offered him a sacrifice and vowed to serve him." ~ Jonah 1:14-16*

You see once I realized that Alonda was a hot mess as they say. I had to make some conscious choices. The first choice that had to be made was I had to learn to cry out just like those sailors for immediate help in the thick of the storm that was the result of someone else's disobedient actions. Remember I mentioned earlier that I had allowed others to lead me off my lighted path of righteousness. My storm was brought about by both the advertent and inadvertent actions of others. Sin crept in because of the way I was reacting to the ungodly actions of those who had betrayed, hurt, offended and rejected me. Secondly, crying out for myself would also help me cancel out the opinions of others, as well as, keep me from persons crying out against me rather than for me... and that subject is a whole different book. Next it was also necessary that I see how imperative it was for me to embrace my difference and accept my assignment. It is my opinion that Jonah didn't want to do either of the two and this is why he was so difficult to train as a Prophet and teach as a believer.

On the flipside the best side, I just love how my God works though because Paul tells us in the book of Romans that all things work together for good to those who love God and are called according to His Purpose. Even in Jonah's disobedience and his pitiful effort to try to out run God. The Sailors who served other god's ended up ditching their false gods and praying to the one True Living God, receiving salvation and becoming servants in the Body of Christ. So I encourage young believers and young prophets in training called to the Purpose of God with this our Father wishes that no man perish, not sinner, saint, and of course not even yourself. I submit to you that your mistakes still have the potential to bring God Glory.

Just look forward to being thrown overboard where the grace of God will show up as a big fish to swallow you. So you can just die already and resurrect with the Power of God that will assist you to walk in obedience no matter where you are assigned to go or who you are assigned to.

I am hopeful that the many who are reading this book will cry out to the only true living God for help like the sailors and if you will as did Jonah whose cry for help is seen in his request to be thrown overboard into the sea. I am telling you it's not until you make your request known to God by hollering out Help throw me overboard. That you will experience a renewed you. The ANOINTED YOU the called to be a FORERUNNER YOU. It's not until you cry out that you will walk in your purpose with both understanding and boldness. You will not experience the favor of God or man until you cry out for help for the removal of the beam in your eye. There is so much more than being mean and miserable. I want the perpetual blessings of God on my life and I would not have come to experience this victorious life had I not sought after the 'Nevertheless' anointing that was on the life of my Savior Jesus Christ.

Saying, Father, if thou be willing, remove this cup from me: <u>nevertheless</u> not my will, but thine, be done." ~ Luke 22:42

There's a saying you can't see the forest for the trees. But one day I got the revelation that it was not trees that were in my way. It was only one tree and that tree was me.

The best way to get out of the way is to give up your permissive will and go after the perfect will of God for your life...Cry out NOW Lord Start with me.

"The best method to stop self-destruction is to stop following your own instruction." ~ Lon

Chapter 4

Back To The Drawing Board - Beams Of Anger, Bitterness, Jealousy, Murder, Pride & Rejection

*"Love is patient, love is kind. It does not
envy, it does not boast, it is not proud.
It does not dishonor others, it is not self-seeking,
it is not easily angered, it keeps no record
of wrongs."~ 1 Corinthians 13:4-5*

❧

So let's talk about how I had allowed rejection to make me bitter and ultimately angry as a bull. Rejection is a generational curse that I inherited. I was told that my paternal grandmother was rejected and looked down on by her very own family. As a child I watched as the spirit of respect of persons cause my earthly dad to go from rejection to ridicule as he suffered a wound from his leaders those he co-labored with in the church and those he loves so very much. Now understanding why that I was a woman with a calling but the exact calling as my dad ultimately the spirit of rejection was spewing over to me the 1st born. I mean it came from the church I grew up in, Sunday school teacher, people I attended school with, so called BFF's, relatives, my parents, in-laws & out laws, old pastors, and even my siblings. In fact I had not realized it was a generational curse until I start writing this chapter. So In the name of Jesus Christ I renounce and denounce the generational curse named rejection and I also prohibit all of rejections cousin spirits depression, dishonor, disgrace, hysteria, anxiety, abuse, bitterness, bashfulness, exile, loneliness and low self-esteem, lack of confidence, hopelessness, emptiness, grandiosity, and introversion to cease from operating in my life Now in Jesus Christ name. I call out and cancel out the assignment of every retaliating spirit of torment, perversion, segregation, suspicions, suicidal ideation, and sabotage, shun and shame. In Jesus Christ Name. AMEN!

Before I go any further let me say this I was fortunate enough to be blessed with GREAT parents. I am more than sure that they don't know that this spirit has operated through them at times. Well once they read this they will know and they know I have no problem explaining it. After all I am their child. The intent of this book is not to bash nor embarrass anyone. This is about my quest for wholeness and my process to become a purged vessel unto honour, sanctified, and meet for the master's use, prepared unto every good work. ~ *2 Timothy 2:21*

Now that that is out of the way back to the scheduled program of Holy Spirit reveals...Although, offense had brought me to this place it had spiraled out of control. The best way to describe what had gripped my heart felt like tentacles were literally stinging and sucking the life out of me. These tentacles of rejection had injected me with the demons of callousness, harshness, bitterness, and slander and ultimately grew into a huge ugly octopus head called ANGER.

"But now was the time to get rid of anger, rage, malicious behavior, slander, and dirty language. - Colossians 3:8. This scripture started the next phase of Help.

First you need to know that most angry people don't know they are angry nor do they desire to stay angry. They just don't understand what anger is, how detrimental it can be or how to get out of it.

❧

What is anger?

Anger is a God given emotion that usually shows up with strong feelings of annoyance, displeasure, and hostility. This emotion is related to one's psychological interpretation of having been offended, wronged, or denied and a tendency to react through retaliation.

Just how dangerous is anger?

This demon of Anger is extremely dangerous it seeks revenge, retaliation, and retribution. It travels closely with the demon spirit murder. If you don't know Hurting People Hurt people. And they often do it without even trying to do so. Oftentimes they are sincere people with sincere efforts but just sincerely wrong.

Signs of an angry person

- they may have cynical malicious speech,
- they can be blatantly disrespectful either in public or private,
- skilled at ignoring you to the point you feel inadequate when you are in their company,
- they will destroy anything in their path including their own possessions,
- and the worst they can become murders if they are never delivered.

I recall one time after either hurricane Katrina or Gustav that my stress level was high and I was extremely more intolerant than my normal personality. Well we had returned back home from evacuating and a few days afterwards I was out running errands. I was enroute to my house when I received a return call from my Insurance agency regarding our homeowners claim. Normally I would not have taken the call but this was extremely important as I answered the call I turned off of the expressway in to the turning lane. In front of me was a police officer. I noticed that he was on the phone at the red light in the turning lane and he wasn't moving. Well I was patiently waiting so I thought because all of the lights were screwed up and being repaired. I even noticed his hands going up in the car but I just thought he was having a heated discussion with someone. I continued to answer the questions of the insurance representative and next thing I know this Caucasian male officer comes up to my car window and begins hollering at me. I mean he was screaming what are you an idiot this lane is closed, I have been telling you to go around. My pot was boiling but in a calm voice I responded to him that I did not know what you were signaling and I thought to get around but it was a little tight to maneuver so I said the smart thing was being patient 'He gets louder no if you get off the x!e@ (expletives) phone and pay attention you could plainly see they are working on the light. Again I responded calmly but in a much more stern and slightly elevated tone "yes sir I am on speakerphone with my insurance representative and again I did not know what you were motioning on the inside of your vehicle. I am fully aware they are working on the traffic signal...(but keep this in mind they were doing that all over and every now and then they'd let cars go thru.) Officer will you assist me in backing up into the oncoming traffic so that I can go around as you requested?" He became even more irate after my last response and answered me

"No you have a license you get over on your own." Ok at this point I knew I was dealing with a retarded and angry demon. I remember thinking to myself if my child was not in this back seat I would cut this fool right on the spot. Lord you gone have to help me. Well in the meantime while he was carrying on and my boiling pot was now on fire the traffic signal began to work properly. Officer went to his car getting ready to pull off and I went around him and turned. Do you know that this angry fool was so mad with me that he sent another officer after me to give me a ticket all because I didn't do it his way. Well my fire turned into a blaze I became an indignant and belligerent somebody with the cordial African American officer who said I should have listened he has to ticket me. "Sir what he was telling me to do was not only dangerous but did not make any sense, and the traffic signal is now fixed so I could turn the vehicles behind me did." Long story short I received a citation and this led to me throwing a fit inside my Mercedes and I destroyed the rearview mirror and damaged the radio. I was so furious that when I saw him pull off while I got cited I said oh I am going to get you sucker. First of all I don't go for men disrespecting women, and this was an officer who had handled me, oh no he isn't getting away with this. I could not see straight I was LIVID. By this time my daughter had called my husband clearly upset because her mom had just went ballistic taking her frustration out on the vehicle. My husband tried but he could not calm me down because I was on my way to find

Mr. Officer as I was hurling death threats at him. I couldn't hear anything my husband was saying I was in a rage and I was all the way over ready to make him feel my wrath. It's bad when no one can get you to come to your senses. Yes, I had an anger issue that was going to end me up in the crazy house because who ain't going to jail is me...lol

I am reminded of the first atrocious murder ever committed and recorded in the world. The biblical account can be found in Genesis chapter four. It is where Adam & Eve's eldest son Cain allowed his anger to fester to the point of murdering his younger brother, Abel.

"When it was time for the harvest, Cain presented some of his crops as a gift to the Lord.⁴ Abel also brought a gift—the best of the firstborn lambs from his flock. The Lord accepted Abel and his gift,⁵ but he did not accept Cain and his gift. This made Cain very angry, and he looked dejected.⁶ "Why are you so angry?" the Lord asked Cain. "Why do you look so dejected?⁷ You will be accepted if you do what is right. But if you refuse to do what is right, then watch out! Sin is crouching at the door, eager to control you. But you must subdue it and be its master."⁸ One day Cain suggested to his brother, "Let's go out into the fields."[c] And while they were in the field, Cain attacked his brother, Abel, and killed him." ~ Genesis 4:3-8

I remember as a youth my first time hearing this story in Sunday school and going Whoa! It is unbelievable how jealousy and intolerance to respect someone's else's progress, pursuit, and passion causes one to become so enraged that they would commit murder rather than celebrate and learn from it. Too often these demons spirits of anger and jealousy has gotten the best of people. The scriptures are clear that God honored Abel's offering because he offered his best. Cain however did not. Yeah pause and think for a moment are you really offering Father your best in your offerings, gifts, talents, and/or your day to day business and activities? Are you upset and covetous over another's offering when you have the same opportunities as they do? Uh huh. A matter of fact are you really giving yourself the best or are you doing yourself an injustice by ignoring the wisdom of the word or even perhaps the wisdom of your mama 'nem? Mull it over in your head for a moment we have the same opportunities to be Obedient, Willing, Cheerful Givers unto the Lord as Abel did. But we often try to be scapegoats, tricksters, corner cutters and jeopardize our relationship with not only God but also amongst one another. This anti-Christ thinking is why far too often we come up short, end up chastised, face embarrassment and harassment and ultimately become embittered. The trip part about this story of these two brothers is Cain committed the double homicide after God warned him that if he didn't check his-self that the sin of anger was going to end up controlling him. His refusal to adhere and decision to hold anger in his bosom didn't just kill Abel but it killed him. Cain's reaction to God landed him a sentence that harmed his entire lineage. He was not only cast out of the presence of God but he would live the rest of his days as a poverty stricken vagabond.

"Then the LORD said to Cain, "Where is your brother Abel? "I don't know," he replied. "Am I my brother's keeper?" The LORD said, "What have you done? Listen! Your brother's blood cries out to me from the ground. Now you are under a curse and driven from the ground, which opened its mouth to receive your brother's blood from your hand. When you work the ground, it will no longer yield its crops for you. You will be a restless wanderer on the earth." Cain said to the LORD, "My punishment is more than I can bear. Today you are driving me from the land, and I will be hidden from your presence; I will be a restless wanderer on the earth, and whoever finds me will kill me."

How many times have you seen the warning signals or been warned that hey you need to check this or that about yourself because this is certainly not a good look but you ignored it. **I believe in my spirit that this is the season that God wants to trust us to Do what is right so that He can respect our offering**. Can you imagine what it would be like to have the Respect of God? To have Him Esteem you and to admire your achievement in walking in wise and Godly counsel. I don't know about you reader but I want the Respect of God so it is a must that I kick out this sin called anger, the enemies called arrogance and ignorance, as well as, anything else hindering me from

becoming perfected in Christ Jesus. Point blank **I am
ready for God to HONOR me for my offerings to Him.**

⧉

What's the remedy for Anger? Just exactly how do I check this sin?

Once again we are to get rid of it as stated in Colossians
3:8 above. We do this by praying strategically to get rid
of the terrible demon named rejection. Then do self-
deliverance on yourself from the spirits of rejection, self-
rejection, and fear of rejection. Don't forget to tell this
demon and its relative anger that it will cease and desist
from ruining your life. You may even have to couple this
along with fasting or enlist a deliverance minister to help
you to loose the bands of wickedness and take authority
of this controlling spirit. *Isaiah chapter 58 and verse six
states this "Is not this the fast that I have chosen? To loose
the bands of wickedness, to undo the heavy burdens, and
to let the oppressed go free, and that ye break every yoke?*
Then Ephesians chapter one verse six tells us to recognize that we are accepted in the beloved. To the praise of
the glory of his grace, wherein he hath made us accepted
in the beloved.

Anger is a God given emotion this is why He tells us
it's okay to be angry however, sin not. We must allow Holy
Spirit to show us how to harness our anger into a righteous

indignation. I had to seek after an encounter with God to help me understand His Love so that I could fulfill His commandment to love, I had to grasp hold to the understanding that God's Love would drive me to have righteous indignation against all sin including my own sin of Anger. I had to constantly remind myself that *Love is patient, love is kind. It does not envy, it does not boast, it is not proud.*[5] *It does not dishonor others, it is not self-seeking, **it is not easily angered**, it keeps no record of wrongs. ~ 1 Corinthians 13:5*

Look you can do this the power of the Holy Spirit does not just make us speak funny, lay hands, and prophesy. He helps us walk in the fruit and liberty of self-control.

We also have to let go because vengeance is the Lords and we are not to touch vengeance. The bible is clear that whatever anyone of us sows we are going to reap. So when someone sows pain, hurt, disrespect and discord God will repay them and show them and they will see your face when they go through it. Oh I remember my reaping season real good. Holy Spirit brings ALL THINGS to your *remembrance...lol.*

Then I had to rest in the fact that Jesus is Healer and Mender He took everything to the cross. Although, when you first experience anguish or if you are like I was my anger was built up from years of suppression. I thought I was like a duck and was letting stuff roll off my back. But when these demon manifestations started showing up I realized that each manifestation was the result of unresolved hurt. I had to allow Holy Spirit to comfort me and even now I have to do it because more and more templates of pain and rejection or showing up than I care to remember. But it's the way to getting set free. Once you allow the Truth to come forth you begin to experience liberty.

Let us pray.

Father help us to not only discern the windows of opportunity to get on the right path but also to decide to take our way of escape called second chance and bring you something You will regard as worthy to bless and use. Right now in the name of Jesus Christ of Nazareth I reject the spirit of Cain now. I vomit up the poison from this venomous spirit. I will bring my flesh into subjection to You Father and cut off the stench of this anti-Christ spirit, I thank you now for giving me keen spiritual sense to identify all things coming in the forms of putrid stubbornness and foul rebellion against you and your word. Right now I choose to embrace and heed to your voice that is gently and lovingly nudging me to the truth of grace to Get It Right and Do It Right. I bind every sign, synergy, symptom, and imp that has been sent out to cause me to reject your truth and cause me to murder my dream or the dreams of others.

I Receive the blessing of Respect and Honor, In Jesus Name – Amen!

Chapter 5

Running Scared – Beam of Intimidation

❧

I mentioned a couple chapters back that God said I was running like the prophet Elijah. Well I like to refer to this season as my next level training. It seemed my life began to pattern like Elijah. See you have to overcome the spirit of intimidation you have so that you can walk in the True Spirit of Elijah which is to Engage in Warfare and Embarrass the Enemy. I had allowed Jezebel to unleash the spirit of intimidation after me to keep me from operating in my anointing as Prophet which is the spirit and power of Elijah, to turn the hearts of the fathers back to the children, and the disobedient to the attitude of the righteous; so as to make ready a people prepared for the Lord." Now how was I going to do that running scared and hiding in caves. I mean every time I obeyed God and He used me to do something supernatural in the earth realm. This witch would come after me and chase me to a cave. She would send out her messengers to tell me you ain't nothing, you ain't do nothing, or I am going to get you for the nothing you just did. She would even send messengers to tell me you are not respected in the Body of Christ nor will I allow you to become known. Well hold up now devil...I had to quickly come to the realization that I have supernatural power and authority over all satanic forces and strange voices coming out of hell. Including this ravenous seductive whore bride of satan named Jezebel. Yes I know I was rough but each word I chose to use is exactly what she is and she has called me worst. Besides that's another volume of books though. Anyway, how is she gone tell me who and what I am. I was enlisted in the heavens for my position before my mother even knew me. I have the greatest one living on the inside of me who gave me the victory through Calvary's cross and left Holy Ghost Power for me. So I had to flip the script to the TRUTH because she knew that I was Impacting, Igniting, & Inspiring lives through Powerful prophetic prayer, prophetic utterances, prophetic gestures and my prophetic function. She knew that I didn't have a complete understanding of my function and that's why she would come after me relentless with her threats from her messenger demons. But early one Sunday morning I rose up in a righteous indignation (properly placed anger) towards her and hell and I evicted the Spirit of Intimidation and declared I would never ever let anyone treat me like I am the curse when I am the blessing. I declared that there was no need for me to run scared because I was already great and called to the Greatest of the Five-fold ascension gifts. Enough was enough I had gotten so intimidated that I no longer waited on her to chase me to the cave. I would automatically run there myself. Holy Spirit had to speak to me and say what are you doing? Stand up directly to this witch and tell her you suffer her not to live, move, nor operate in your life, business, or affairs. I began to strike down every chant, word curse, and death threat she sent to me and my God given assignment. I even stopped her seeking and scanning spirits from reporting back to her and the satanic council. I stopped them from peeping in on my prayers, conversations, and plans so that they could no longer hinder me in my assignment. **Warning:** You have to deal with yourself honestly so you can deal with this enemy spirit.

Ya see, as a Prophet, Seer, and Perceiver I had to come to an end of my flesh and become spiritual...that's right young Prophets you must become obedient unto death.

"And being found in fashion as a man, he humbled himself, and became obedient unto death, even the death of the cross."~ Philippians 2:8

Chapter 6

Even More Beams

❈

The truth is we have more beams to deal with than we care to admit or can actually count most times. But I will deal with the few that Holy Spirit has helped or is yet helping me to eradicate. I am sure that if you would be honest you will agree that most of your beams are rebellion, lack of patience, double mindedness, wicked or wounded heart, and the mighty unruly double tongue.

First, let me make sure we understand that rebellion is resistance, defiance and opposition to one in authority or dominance; Open, armed, and usually unsuccessful defiance of or resistance to an established governing authority.

Boy it's going to definitely require some exercised patience to get this beam out of your eye. Look at it this way you will get to deal with two at one time. This booger rebellion is so bad the bible references it as the sin of witchcraft. Mmmm, Makes you shout ouch doesn't it? Because you know that while you are trying to criticize others and find fault with others. You are rebelling against the word of God yourself. God says love you hate, God said bring your tithes and offerings, to the storehouse and you just stay home to watch TV online. Husbands & Wives you should be submitting one to another but instead you ignore and disrespect each other. What about this obey the laws of the land but somewhere or somehow we go over the speed limit and straight thru traffic signals or maybe you just skip the petty misdemeanors and go for the gusto and cheat on your taxes. Children obey your parents for this is right it's the first commandment with promise. But yet you rebel and forfeit your blessings.

Then there is the issue of patience. We want everyone to be patient with us because God's not through with us. But yet and still we have low tolerance for others who are going through their grooming and pruning season or while they learn to work out their soul salvation. All of us need to really evaluate ourselves for these beams and deal with them in our own lives lest we be castaways and become isolated by both man and God.

What do you think of when you hear the word beam? Well, when I think of beam I think of the towering electric poles. Now any genius or fool can readily see that not only are electric poles tall but they are heavy in density and weight. Allow yourself to Release others and begin ridding yourself of the weight of ALL your own beams.

God doesn't want us weighed down He wants us to be Lite and to be the Light. **In order to become an innocuous and unthreatening version of you, you're going to have to cast the care and burdens of beams on Him.** We shouldn't be carrying these loads especially in our small eye sockets. Carrying these beams in our eyes impairs our vision to love as Christ Loves and to receive what God has not only for us through us but also the blessing that can come from the others that we are so impatient with, disloyal to, dislike and rebel against. I hope you're getting it because I don't know how to make it any clearer. It is said that the eyes are the light of the soul or the spirit of a man. Many have dim or no light left in their eyes because of the beams. We should have energy exuding from us to help us see things. After all, light is what makes vision possible. Some of you will catch that later.

HEART Beam –

We have to be real careful with this one because this is the place where the issues of life flow out of and boy oh boy sometimes when you listen to people or perhaps even yourself you will discover more often than not that nothing is flowing from the heart of man but sludge and drudge. Yes the Drudgery of wickedness, heart break, Sludge of bitterness, Contempt, and Rebellion. The heart can become so hard until it will cause one to take on what I call the bastard syndrome. I do not want to assume everyone knows the definition of bastard so here goes: A bastard usually has to do with illegitimacy, or someone that is spurious not authentic, genuine, or sincere and we all know by context clues that it can also be someone who is mean spirited or disagreeable or questionable. Don't close the book on me because I used the word bastard to describe many or even maybe yourself, but after careful observation of others but more importantly myself, I found that I was not only living like an illegitimate child but I was becoming just as insincere and sinister as those who I had once admired and loved. Instead of offering a genuine smile I had taught my heart to lie and offered no more than a halfhearted grin which is really what I call the hurt smirk or the phony smile. My character was in question by Holy Spirit. Bastard Syndrome had me responding as if I was the spawn of satan rather than like one who was adopted and accepted. I was holding so much in my heart. I may not have indulged in public or private smear campaigns but I was holding a many a prisoner in my heart. I had become so contemptuous. The truth is by definition many have taken on the bastard syndrome because the beams were not just in their eyes but had also taken root in the heart. The heart the place that is designed to pump our life line our blood flow through is now bogged down by these heavy beams. The heart although small and tough is still yet very delicate and intricate. Naturally if anything begins to block any part of the heart. The heart begins to experience stress, strain, and struggle. We all know that if there is blockage in the heart then the quality of life is diminished, as well as, it will be inevitable that death will arise. Well same thing spiritually anytime we allow the enemy of our soul to cause the splinters from beams to pierce our heart and block the flow of the anointing of God's Love in our lives. Our hearts are becoming harder day by day. The bible tells us that man looks at the outer appearance but He looks at the heart. On the outside you may look like your heart is functioning properly. But God is saying 'Oh no it's way past time for you to deal with your heart issues and dissolve these heart blockages.' Well at least that's what He has being doing to me over the years, reminding me constantly to keep my heart pure so that I could see Him (GOD/Jesus). See King David had a clear understanding of this that is why he cried out Create in me a Clean Heart. **We can't see or trust God unless our hearts are clear of beguile, foolishness, and hate**. These splinters will keep us from experiencing God like He desires us to. These splinters will keep us from receiving the very desires of our own heart. So in this I am teaching you the importance of guarding your heart. Satan knows that there are so many benefits to receive from heaven that is why he is always trying to keep us feeling flustered, frustrated, berated, and degraded. He keeps us in uproars over frivolous nonessential things like he looked at me wrong. She didn't speak to you, oh they could have acknowledge you but you see you don't have what they have so that's why you are never invited. Just all kinds of stupid stuff and when we are not on guard where our hearts are concerned before you know it you will have blocked your heart with a beam or two or three. So start praying *Father let the words of my mouth and the meditations of my heart be pleasing and acceptable in your sight. My Strength and My redeemer. ~ Psalm 19:14*

DOUBLE MIND Beam –

If I haven't unloaded enough on you to contemplate change wait to you read the next beam that I recently had to eradicate. Holy Spirit one day spoke so gently to me you're becoming unstable because you didn't deal with the root cause of many issues, because of your refusal to be confrontational regarding certain aspects of your life, as well as, certain people. After not being able to see or agree right away with what He had revealed. He showed me where I was lacking the mind of Christ and I had lost my zeal and optimism. Unbeknownst to me I had become a faithful member of The Church of Pessimism. You know where you believe the doctrine that reality is evil and that evil trumped happiness in life. Oh I spent days and months preaching sermons to myself about the worst outcomes, adverse conditions and aspects on possibilities.

Yes me a woman of faith an ordained clergyman. I had faith for others but I was running empty for myself. After Holy Spirit bringing all things to my remembrance, repenting and prayer this is the counsel I received from heaven.

REMEDY FOR THE DOUBLE MIND

"*Draw near to God* and He will draw near to you. *Cleanse your hands*, *you* sinners; and *purify your hearts*, *you* double-minded." ~ James 4:8

Let's revisit the story of Jonah and see how as a Prophet he walked in double mindedness and was quite unstable....Jonah in the latter chapters gets to Nineveh and vacillates and becomes upset because God changes His mind about killing the people. Ok Jonah why are you so stiffed neck and why are you so vengeful why don't you want anybody else to experience God's Grace, Mercy, and Power. To those of us who have experienced deep wounds or who have not dealt with the spirit of selfishness. Holy Spirit showed me how the logs of wounds and selfishness and the double minded beam brought about an infidelity, faithlessness in God. I needed to change my perspective as it related to others who were lost both in the church & out. As well as, about my present circumstance. After all, He is no respecter of person and He doesn't need me to decide that someone else doesn't deserve another chance nor that I didn't or that I did. I began to comprehend that if I did not dilate my eyesight and grab hold of my mind that my instability was going to cause me to be a stumbling block to many and I was not going to receive the restitution that was to come to me. I began to see how beams form ugly scar tissues obstructing one's vision of them self, others and more importantly even God.

I think this is a great spot to pray a quick prayer.

> *Father, I want to be like minded with heaven having the same love and one accord. Show me in my fellowship with you Holy Spirit how to esteem others better including myself. Let this mind be in me that was also in Christ Jesus. Holy Spirit teach me and help me be obedient even until death. In Jesus Christ name, Amen*

∞

TONGUE Beam –

And lastly, the absolute worst beam was my TONGUE. I know you are thinking I am going to talk about being flippant again. But I am actually going to cover it differently. I kept hearing in my spirit unruly member. Pastoring alongside my husband and being an intercessor I immediately thought oh I better right that down so He can show me who it is as I rolled my neck. I earnestly sought to know who the unruly member was so that I can pray strategic targeted prayer of deliverance. Whelp, the only thing I got was, *"no daughter rectify your tongue it is an unruly member of your body."* Let's look at the word of God that Holy Spirit led me to meditate on.

Even so the tongue is a little member, and boasteth great things. Behold, how great a matter a little fire kindleth!⁶ And the tongue is a fire, a world of iniquity: so is the tongue among our members, that it defileth the whole body, and setteth on fire the course of nature; and it is set on fire of hell.⁷ For every kind of beasts, and of birds, and of serpents, and of things in the sea, is tamed, and hath been tamed of mankind:⁸ But the tongue can no man tame; it is an unruly evil, full of deadly poison. ~ James 3:5-8

If we aren't careful our tongues will burn up our destiny, and start the funeral arrangements for the prophecy over our lives.

In order to be cured of all that was ailing me in the natural I was going to have to correct the way I was utilizing my tongue. I took a week and examined the conversations I was having in my mind, my heart, as well as, with others and found that I had set my tongue in motion with nihilism the viewpoint that makes destruction viable and eliminates all constructive possibilities. This surely was not of God and I was over the same old same old. I was committing suicide and homicide with this member.

REMEDY FOR THE TONQUE

I had to retrain my mouth to alleviate the troubles I had caused because of my skepticism and emptiness. I am becoming more disciplined in not allowing any corrupt communication to drop out of my mouth that would cause me anguish. In other words I stopped saying I am broke. I started speaking wealth and riches are in my house and wisdom has come with it. I only use words to build up my house, husband, kids, and ministry. Even when it's a prophetic word or rebuke, I do not change the word of the Lord but I make it understood that it is His love for us that He visit us and chides us on occasion.

Jesus even stated in Matthew 15:11 that it was not what goes into the mouth that defiles a person but what comes out of the mouth that defiles a person.

NOW IS THE TIME FOR YOU TO STOP allowing the tongue beam to taint your life and start allowing it to paint your life. Unclean and impure speech absorbed by you and directed toward others really doesn't solve anything but it does present problems. THE MAIN PROBLEMS BEING DEATH AND CURSES. Here's how I started choosing Life and Blessings.

I began to pray Psalm 141:3 and ask Father to set a guard over my mouth and keep watch over the door of my lips. Holy Spirit quicken me that no corrupt words will be released into the earth that would kill my purpose or Gods plan for me. I began to declare and decree that I would not only choose life but love life, I used this member to make the declaration that I would see good days therefore my tongue would no longer be permitted to speak evil and I vowed to refrain from deceit. I am learning how to use my tongue to give life and be life by speaking with acumen, inspiration, incitement and wisdom. They tell me by nature that I am witty so I even had to hone in on my humor to ensure that I was building even in laughter. Besides as James stated in James chapter three a teacher would be judged more strictly so Sister Girl had to get it together. I don't want to be tying up the line in heaven trying to explain why I said what I said on Judgment day. All I want to here is your 100,000 square foot mansion is over here. Oh and for you deep religious folks servant well done gone sound good to my ears to.

    *See Appendix for scriptures on the tongue and mouth

Conclusion

"We are all a work in progress however the
problem is to many of us are out to recess
instead of completing the process." ~ Lon

⚜

My quest for success and desire to please God my
Father not only generated my cry for Help but also
yielded a YES Lord here I am send me. But before you can
really fulfill purpose in your life one of these days you are
going to have to see the Lord and when you do see him.
You will say as the Prophet Isaiah said

*"Woe is me, for I am undone! Because I am a man of
unclean lips, And I dwell in the midst of a people of unclean
lips; For my eyes have seen the King, The Lord of hosts. ~
Isaiah 6:5*

**and then you will experience the liberty
of purification and sanctification.**

Then one of the seraphim flew to me, having in his hand a live coal which he had taken with the tongs from the altar. And he touched my mouth with it, and said: "Behold, this has touched your lips; Your iniquity is taken away, And your sin purged." ~ Isaiah 6:6-7

Next, I would like to conclude with these scriptures because this is where my demand for help bought me. So take a Selah (pause) moment, reflect, meditate and memorize them.

"I have been crucified with Christ. It is no longer I who live, but Christ who lives in me. And the life I now live in the flesh I live by faith in the Son of God, who loved me and gave himself for me." ~ Galatians 2:20

*"He staggered not at the promise of God through unbelief; but was **strong** in faith, giving glory to God; And being fully persuaded that, what he had promised, he was able also to perform." ~ Romans 4:20-21*

"I am not ashamed of who I am, for I know whom I have believed, and I am fully persuaded that He is able to keep me, no matter what may happen to me or where I may find myself. I know God is the One who called me and that He is able to take me to the fulfillment of His purpose." ~ 2 Timothy 1:12

My final prayer is that all who read this book become crucified with Christ and that the life you live Now is by faith in the Son of God who loves you and gave himself for you. I hope that your comprehension has been expanded to determination to submit to the counsel of Holy Spirit who will help you change how you See, Say, and Pray. I ask Father to feed you your daily bread of deliverance and bless you richly with all spiritual blessing, keen discernment, and reward you for your diligence in working out your soul salvation with fear and trembling for Him. In Jesus Christ Name, Amen

Appendix

❋

Scriptural References:

Proverbs 21:23 Whoever keeps his mouth and his tongue keeps himself out of trouble.

Ephesians 4:29 Let no corrupting talk come out of your mouths, but only such as is good for building up, as fits the occasion, that it may give grace to those who hear.

James 1:26 If anyone thinks he is religious and does not bridle his tongue but deceives his heart, this person's religion is worthless

Proverbs 15:4 A gentle tongue is a tree of life, but perverseness in it breaks the spirit

Psalm 37:30 The mouth of the righteous utters wisdom, and his tongue speaks justice

Proverbs 10:19 When words are many, transgression is not lacking, but whoever restrains his lips is prudent

References used: ONLINE BIBLES – Amplified, ESV, New KING James Version, New Living Translation, NIV or The Message Bible. All Rights reserved ©

Note from Author:

From the bottom of my heart I want to express a sincere thank you for purchasing my first published book and I certainly hope you enjoyed and were affected in a positive light. Now I invite you to keep in touch with me by visiting my website www.alondacooper.com where I have more awesome products, news, and for bookings.

Love,

Lon

www.ingramcontent.com/pod-product-compliance
Lightning Source LLC
Chambersburg PA
CBHW060424050426
42449CB00009B/2116